OSAMEDE ARHUNMWUNDE

HIGHER
EDUCATION
101

Understanding the secrets
to personal development

 **FriesenPress**

Suite 300 – 990 Fort Street
Victoria, BC, Canada V8V 3K2
www.friesenpress.com

Copyright © 2014 by Osamede Arhunmwunde
First Edition — 2014

ISBN
978-1-4602-4532-3 (Hardcover)
978-1-4602-4533-0 (Paperback)
978-1-4602-4534-7 (eBook)

1. Self-Help, General

Distributed to the trade by The Ingram Book Company

1   Introduction

5   Chapter One

9   Chapter Two
    Fundamentals: MAN

19 Chapter Three
    Revelation

25 Chapter Four
    The Power of Association

31 Chapter Five
    Action

35 Chapter Six
    Goals

47 Chapter Seven
    Your Why

55 Chapter Eight
    Share

61 Conclusion
    Change Your World

"Our deepest fear is not that we are inadequate. Our deepest fear is that we are powerful beyond measure. It is our light, not our darkness, that most frightens us. We ask ourselves, who am I to be brilliant, gorgeous, talented and fabulous? Actually, who are you not to be? You are a child of God. Your playing small doesn't serve the world.

We were born to make manifest the glory of God that is within us. It's not just in some of us; it's in everyone. And as we let our own light shine, we unconsciously give other people permission to do the same.

As we are liberated from our own fear, our presence automatically liberates others."

Marianne Williamson
(b. 1952)

INTRODUCTION

MY JOURNEY to personal development started as a young boy searching for the formula for success.

On this journey I met many teachers and philosophers who spoke of many things about our elusive world. One of the most profound was their definition of success: they taught me and instructed me on the principles of success and how to achieve it.

Like the laws of nature, the laws of gravity, and the laws of physics; the true principles of success and the keys to understanding who we are and what our purpose here on Earth is have been with us for thousands of years. These principles have never changed. And as I see it, are going to work for you or against you regardless of what you do or who you are.

We are living in a crazy age, so we believe we have to have fast answers, easy solutions, and free lunches. In looking for this quick fix to our challenges, we have become so blinded to old principles that have always worked and always will work. Even though they are right under our nose, we don't see them anymore so we think of them as secrets.

On my extraordinary adventure to success, I have been learning the secret of personal development. As one of my teachers put it: "It is the challenge to develop ourselves and our skills to see what we can create in the way of value." Value makes the difference in result.

I believe personal development, or to become more valuable, is the key to all good things. This belief has revolutionized my life. Of all the things that can have an effect on your future, I believe personal development is the greatest. The great axiom of life as my mentor once said is: "You can have more than you've got because you can become more than you are."

The major key to your better future is you. That is what this book is all about; understanding who you really are, and how to create the life you want. What you become influences what you get and true happiness is not contained in what you get; as I see it, happiness is contained in what you become.

An old Japanese tale tells of a mountain in central Japan, with a flattened plateau at the top, surrounded by a dense jungle. According to the tale, the mountain was called: "The place where you leave your parents." If one's parents reached a certain age and they were still alive, their children carried them through the jungle, to the top of the mountain and left them there for the gods.

The tale tells us of a young man, headed right for the mountain, fighting his way through the underbrush carrying a little old lady on his strong shoulders. He carried on and as they climbed higher, he noticed she was doing something with her hands. Finally, he looked up at her, half in anger and half in guilt, and asked her "Mother what are you doing?"

The old lady looked down at her son and answered with tears streaming down her wrinkled cheeks, yet her eyes were filled only with love for her son, " Son I am just breaking off a few branches and dropping them to mark a path so that after you leave me, you will be able to find your way back home. Sooner or later I suppose someone will be taking me up to my mountain but before they do, if you let me, I would like to break a couple of branches for you".

As you read this book, remember you don't have to buy into everything any one person says. Although, I suggest you do yourself a favour and keep an open mind because just like a parachute, our minds work best when it is open and remember ... don't be a follower, be a student.

CHAPTER ONE

PERSONAL DEVELOPMENT: There are three parts to personal development that you need to understand and work on.

Self-education, the ability to act, and the unique ability to share.

Self-education

The word "education" has always fascinated me; what it means; how it applies to us as a humanity; and, its role in our personal growth. I grew up in a family that held "schooling and an education" as important for many good reasons. But for me, the education system failed to help build my passion or explain my curiosity. It served as a guideline for a pre-meditated set of goals from which I had to choose.

The system was not focused on helping me to build my gifts and abilities to fulfil my purpose, but was preparing me to fit into the already set goals. I was on my way to one of these pre-set goals when I met my first teacher; Dove Brown.

I worked for her in my university days and she opened my mind to a whole new world of possibilities. I shared with her my ambitions and goals and she explained that in order to go where I wanted in life and maximize my potential, I needed to be re-educated, and be self-educated. She introduced me to new teachers and thinkers through books and she coached me in the first couple years of my self-education journey. Ever since then my hunger to understand life and maximize my potential has never seized. Consequently, I was able to redefine my purpose in life and walk towards it.

My journey has been filled with challenges, but as a friend rightly said, "What are challenges if not building blocks."

Muscle growth occurs whenever the rate of muscle protein buildup is greater than the rate of muscle protein breakdown, but the breakdown starts the process that leads to the build up. Nonetheless, the breakdown (most times) is accompanied by pain, but the results are stronger and bigger muscles. So are life challenges, they can be painful and they can break us down, but they also force new growth: stronger growth if we don't give up.

A young spoken word artist by the name Suli Breaks wrote a piece entitled: *Why I Hate School but Love Education.* Among many things, I was inspired by one of his sentences: "Redefine how you view education and understand its true meaning."

That got me thinking as to how many people actually understand the true meaning of education. Most of the time we assume the schooling system to be all there is to education. You see education etymologically is derived from a Latin word édúcó (to draw out, to develop from within).

According to a mentor of mine, an educated person is not necessarily one who has an abundance of general or specialized knowledge. Educated people have developed the faculties of their minds so that they may acquire anything they want, without violating the rights of others. Educated people are curious people who have learnt to study how things work; they know who they are and understand their life purpose and have gone to work on them. They are people who let their environment touch them; they absorb from everything around them and take action.

History has proved that the best-educated people are those who are self-educated. It takes more than a university degree to make one a person of education. You see, I made a commitment to become an educated man. I truly believe becoming self-educated is a key to personal growth.

Self-education requires that you study how things work in your environment. Study the things that can change your life, but in order to do this you have to become a good reader. Do everything you can and find out all you can do.

An ancient script says: "Study to show thyself approved."

Standard education will get you standard results. But why not go beyond the standard and become the extraordinary? Become an above average person and you will have an above average life. Education is preparation.

As Abraham Lincoln (1809-1865) said: "If I had six hours to chop down a tree, I'd spend the first four hours sharpening the axe."

Self-education is a lifelong process and should only end when we do.

CHAPTER TWO
FUNDAMENTALS: MAN

THE FIRST part in self-education is to truly understand "who you are". There are many theories and ideas out there that make many claims to "who you are", but as I shared earlier on, don't be a follower, be a student.

It's important to know your identity, without this, you can be lost and spend all your life meandering in a maze of mediocrity. One of my mentors once taught me that the wealthiest place in the world is not the oil fields of Iran, nor the diamond mines or gold mines of South Africa, or Fort Knox in Kentucky, but in graveyards.

He explained that graveyards contain the human potential that was never discovered. For example, great music that was never written; poems that could have changed the world that were never told; inventions that were never discovered; paintings that were never painted; great men who died as poor men and alcoholics; leaders that died as followers; ideas and dreams of multitude of people that are forever buried in graveyards because they never truly lived life. And, as I see it, one of the major reasons was a lack of identity.

I grew up in a spiritual household and taught that the spiritual precedes the physical, and an understanding of the spiritual would explain a lot of what we see in the physical. However, growing up as a child I had ideas of my own that didn't include the spiritual. As an adult, when I got into the business world, I discovered that most successful business men had some sort of an edge that gave them an added advantage over everyone else. Now this "edge" wasn't something reserved for the "rich and famous", it was available to everyone who would ask, seek and knock in persistence at the door of understanding.

An ancient script says: "Get wisdom, get understanding: forget it not; neither decline from the words of my mouth. Forsake her not, and she shall preserve thee: love her, and she shall keep thee. Wisdom is the principal thing; therefore get wisdom: and with all thy getting get understanding. Exalt her, and she shall promote thee: she shall bring thee to honour, when thou dost embrace her. She shall give to thine head an ornament of grace: a crown of glory shall she deliver to thee."

Those are very powerful words if you understand them. I quickly realized I needed an edge and a series of events led me to an ancient book written many, many years ago. During the early stage of my personal growth, I was introduced to many "teachers of old" and I studied them and their philosophies. I soon began to see a trend. The majority of them seemed to refer to the spiritual world, or the cosmos as "the source" of all energy and that the higher spiritual powers can create anything from nothing, and how we are all connected to one another and to this infinite power. They all agreed that within us there is something that connects us to the divine.

In a lot of their texts they do not elaborate on this power, nor explain the mechanics of which it operates. It's almost as though they gave us blanks to be filled by our own self-education, or perhaps they didn't want to scare people away with all of the truth because the "reality" we live in seems so different that it would be hard to fully understand and accept a new world.

The uneducated mind (most times) can be scared of that which it doesn't understand. However, I remembered my mentor saying: "Great teachers inspire you, and give you insight to stimulate your hunger to know more. They do not give answers; they show you where to find them. Nothing is yours until you discover it."

Curiosity lead me to ask, seek, and knock on the door of understanding. In time I was lead to an ancient book: this book held so many secrets and filled in "the blanks" in a lot of what my teachers had been trying to teach me about the world we live in and how it operates; about our connection to this infinite power; and what it is that we have in us that can make us achieve anything we believe with conviction and go to work on.

Over the years, the "powers that be" have tried to hide this book; fought the truth contained in the book; and even tried to corrupt this book for many years. However, the underlying message remained and only those who truly seek its knowledge and wisdom will see it between the pages.

Nothing I share with you is new: It's all old information. My teacher once told me "Be wary of a man who says he has 'new' fundamentals".

Fundamentals are old. It's the man who says, "Come check out this big plant we have, we manufacture antiques."

I advise you to be wary. Everything I share with you here is old truth. First promulgated by the great teachers and philosophers of old time fame.

In regards to personal development, understanding who you are is the starting point. Understanding your identity is fundamental: it is the starting place for true personal growth and just like every other one of life's fundamental, it doesn't change, it has been the same for thousands of years. Many teachers have found other ways to say it, but the message is the same. Personal growth all starts with understanding who you are as a human.

A lot of these ideas are primarily from the Bible, the ancient book I discovered a long time ago that contains the secrets of the worlds. Now, I am not a theologian or minister, but in my journey to personal growth I have found the Bible to be an excellent guide for ideas and success equations. As I see it, this book is not a religious book nor is it to exalt any religion: but the Bible is as practical as it is spiritual and was written for people of all backgrounds and beliefs who want to know the truth and grow to live and enjoy the higher life. For your sake, may you become like a little child with eagerness to learn.

In Genesis 1:26, we read "And God said, let us make man in our image, after our likeness ... and let them have dominion."

This script contains the secret to truly answering the age-old question: "Who am I?"

You see "man" is the name God gave to the spirit being. We are all man or have man inside of us; we might have a different body. For example, regardless of gender, we are all man. Man is spirit and is our connection to the divine. This is why the Bible never really makes reference to male or female; God usually addresses man. In John 4:2 we read: "God is spirit: and they that do business with him must come in spirit and in sincerity."

The true essence of man is spirit and in the spiritual realm there's neither male nor female, neither black nor white, neither Greek nor Jew: these are all "dirt or flesh" related. We are all one spirit. My life revolutionized when I understood this truth.

Now, we were created in the image of God. The Hebrew meaning of the word "image" refers to have been created in the nature of God, to be naturally like God. If you sincerely want to know who you should be like and want to understand who you are, you must study God. Whatever is unnatural for God is unnatural for you. For example, God is never afraid; so fear for man is unnatural; it is something we have taught ourselves. We read in Paul's message to Timothy: "God has not given us the spirit of fear; but of power, and of love and of a sound mind."

We were created to function in the likeness of God. You see, God functions by faith. Faith in the ancient scripts was defined as: "The substance of things hoped for, the evidence of things not seen."

This is another revolutionary idea. You see, God created the world by faith and daily we create our world through faith. You have within you the power to function just like God. This is why we become what we continually say and believe about ourselves. It works whether you believe it or not. You see, there are two ways to see: you can see with your eyes and you can see with your mind. Your eyes will see things, but your mind will see answers. When you understand this, you will learn to never say what you see, but say what you desire.

Right now you live in a world that you created with your mouth and mind. This is exactly how God created the world, by speaking it into being. And in the same way, every day you create your own world.

And finally we were created to have dominion: to rule, to master, to lead. Every human was created to dominate in life: not to dominate over one another, but over the domain of your gifting. We were all created with a specific area of gifting and you are supposed to master that area; dominate that area; lead in that area; and have authority in that area of gifting; and that is where you are supposed to impact the world through.

My teacher once said: "Work harder on yourself, work harder on your gifts than you do on your job."

You compete against you. There's an African proverb that says: "If there's no enemy within, the enemy without can do us no harm."

In Proverbs 18:16 we read: "A man's gift makes room for him and brings him before kings."

The first step to personal growth is to realize that you have the spirit nature of God; and have been created to function like God; and to have his characteristics and dominate a particular gifting; and finally, to be a king.

"If the universe is an accident, then we are accidents but if there is meaning in the universe, there is meaning in us too."

CHAPTER THREE

REVELATION

THE SECOND part in self-education is to discover your purpose. Purpose is defined as the original reason for creation. We have to trust the basic principle that nothing exists in this universe without a pre-destined life; everything on this universe was created to serve a purpose. My mentor once said: "The greatest tragedy in life is not death; the greatest tragedy in life is life without a purpose. It is more tragic than death. It is more tragic to be alive and not know why, than to be dead and not know life. A dead man doesn't have to give a reason for his day."

These powerful words stirred up my spirit to go in search for my purpose and that in itself, began my next level in personal development. I realized that it is our life purpose that helps us stay disciplined through the personal growth process and demands that we set standards for living.

In Proverbs 29:18, we read: "Where there is no vision, the people perish."

This will explain why many people are frustrated with life. You see, we were created to live a life filled with meaning and purpose and to have passion for what we do: not just to live and earn a living or get by in life. As I see it, fulfilment will only come from discovering your purpose and walking in it. What a frustration it must be to live a life without any meaning or without knowing our true potential and purpose. Man was not created as an experiment: there was a plan.

The good Lord said to Jeremiah: "Before I formed you in the womb I knew you."

There are no surprises in this universe. You and I are on a mission in this universe; we have been sent from eternity into time for a designated purpose to make a deposit to our generation; to influence and share our gifts with the world.

Earlier on, I told of the story my mentor shared with me about the wealthiest place on Earth; he also told me that the wealth of the graveyard is called potential. Potential as a noun means abilities that may be developed and lead to future success or unused success; it's dormant power. This is what we all carry inside of us that can transform our lives into one of meaning.

We need to work on our abilities; maximize our present abilities. Do not die with your dreams inside you; do not die and become part of the graveyard; or die on empty. Give all your gifts and abilities to the world.

My mentor showed me that the bible also shows us the principle of potential in nature. In Genesis 1:11 we read: "And God said, Let the earth bring forth grass, the herb yielding seed, and the fruit tree yielding fruit after his kind, whose seed is in itself, upon the earth: and it was so."

Every seed has trapped within it a tree and most importantly the next generation of trees. The world is made up of principles, eternal truths that are fixed just like the principle of gravity. The seed of everything is hiding away in itself. This suggests that the creator hides the potential of a human being inside man. This is why Solomon, King of Israel said in a proverb: "It is the glory of God to conceal a matter; to search out a matter is the glory of Kings." This is why you need to get to know God; you need to know what he knows about you.

Your future is not out in the world, it is but within you. The future of a seed is not in the soil, but within the seed. You are valuable to the world. It has been said that 90 out of 100 people do not have a major purpose in life: as I see it, this is not true. Every human being has a major purpose in life. Every man was especially designed to serve the world in some particular channel.

Ninety percent of humanity has not discovered their channel. The very word "individual" suggests that we are all uniquely different from one another and we should appreciate our own individual design. For example, our fingerprints are unique, there is no other living being with our fingerprint.

The greatest teacher of all reminded us that even the very hairs on our heads have been numbered. That reveals how much detail was put into our creation.. The teacher from the plains of Galilee also said: "Ask and it will be given to you; seek and you will find; knock and the door will be opened to you. For everyone who asks receives; the one who seeks finds; and the one who knocks, the door will be opened."

If you are feeling down and not quite sure what your purpose on Earth is, perhaps your first goal at this time should be to search out what you are passionate about; what you would do not for money; but for the satisfaction that comes from fulfilment. If you still need more clarity, then ask that you be shown what your purpose on Earth is. Who do you ask? Ask God, the omnipotent. Remember, we are all connected to the infinite intelligence. We can access this power through the subconscious phase of our mind in prayer, but you must ask in sincerity.

CHAPTER FOUR
THE POWER OF ASSOCIATION

THE THIRD part to self-education is the power of association. My advice: be very careful of your associations. The power of association needs to be understood and implemented; the people you spend the most time with are going to have a larger impact on your life than you could possibly imagine. You will become the average of those whom you spend the most of your time with and, if you're not conscious, they can influence you positively or negatively.

There was a scientist who did a study on fleas. He placed half a dozen fleas in a glass canister, to observe, and immediately placed a lid on the glass canister. What did the fleas do in times of crisis? They jumped. When fleas jump, it's no ordinary leap. They can shoot as high as 100 times their body length, and horizontally up to 13 inches. The fleas kept trying to jump out of the canister over and over again, but every time they would hit against the lid. As he watched them jump, something became obvious. The fleas continued to jump, but they no longer jumped high enough to hit the lid.

After about an hour, the scientist was able to take the lid off the canister and the fleas continued to jump, but they never jumped out of the canister. Fleas are one of the best jumpers of all known insects relative to their body size. They are born and designed to jump 13 inches, but now they couldn't jump four inches. After they hit their heads several times, they decided to still jump, but not as high and since none of the other conditioned fleas were willing to try again to jump out: they all just remained trapped in their self-imposed limitation.

The amazing thing about the study is this; as soon as the scientist introduced a new flea into the canister (a flea that didn't know there was a limit to what it can do or how high it can jump) the flea jumped back out and the rest of the conditioned fleas also began to jump back out.

They got their vision back. That's an example of what people can do to us: they can either cause us to remain trapped in self-imposed limitations or give us back our vision. People are like elevators; they would either take you up or bring you down.

My mentor once told me: "If you cannot change your friends, change your friends."

I personally pick my associations in the books I read. I have found as little as 30 minutes a day of reading a good positive book that inspires, instructs, and challenges me is a great foundation to becoming self-educated and employing the power of association. As I see it, for personal growth, you have to be a good reader. Thus, on your journey to personal development, you have to learn to stay curious, just like a child. But again: remember to be a student and not a follower.

While I was growing up, I always heard the phrase: "Experience is the best teacher." What they failed to add to that phrase is: "We don't live long enough to gain all the experiences needed to live the higher life."

Many philosophers and teachers have condensed 50-plus years of life experiences into books and all we have to do is pick them up and read. The solution is easy; all a person has to do is to learn from other people's experiences. Do you realize there are people who have been through similar challenges as yourself? There are people who have successfully discovered their life's purpose. There are people who have successfully navigated their way through their journey, live the life they want and have documented their journeys in books.

Did you know that hundreds of successful people have documented how they achieved their success in books? Did you know that there are books that teach you how to live a higher life? Did you know that there are books written to help you identify your life purpose? Reading books can save you years of hard knock life experience. If you read them: allow the past, great philosophers and teachers to be your teachers.

To be self-educated we need a consistent plan for acquiring knowledge; this is especially why I keep a library of great thinkers. I believe what a man reads pours ingredients into his mind and his life is built and shaped by his mind. If you spend time reading trash, you can't build a rich dynamic positive life. You have to select the kind of materials that can build your mind. It doesn't matter where you get the bad stuff from, it doesn't matter who gives it to you; it will still do its damage.

To do better, you have to be around the right people. Never underestimate the power of influence. Whether you know it or not, whoever you are around exerts some influence on you. So make sure you around the right set of people who are growing and changing. Get around the right people that can help to make your life better on a constant and consistent basis. Everyday you have to stand guard at the door of your mind. Don't allow just anything in because you will have to live with the results for the rest of your life and we only get to live once.

Like they say in the field of computer science: Garbage in, garbage out.

CHAPTER FIVE

ACTION

THE SECOND part to personal development is consistent practice; developing the ability to take action and have the ability to act. After we have discovered who we are and why we are here on Earth; and studied and learnt how life works; we must go to work.

There is no telling what you can do today if you really wish to. The human capacity has never really been the problem; it is not a matter of capacity but of will and wanting something "too bad enough". Nothing can take the place of action.

In the words of Bruce Lee (1940-1973): "Knowing is not enough, we must apply, willing is not enough, we must do".

There is ancient script that says: "Faith without action is dead."

I couldn't say it any better. Study without discipline and action is the beginning of delusion. Study and inspiration must lead to discipline and action. Action creates value and value makes the difference in result. You must be able to make your flesh do the things necessary to achieve your life purpose and it's as easy as doing the little things daily like setting goals. For example (as mentioned above), reading 20 minutes of a good book, both for the result in changing something in your life and for the mental muscle.

Did you know that if you read 20 minutes a day of a good and positive book and you are an average reader? At the end of the year you would have read 20 - 200 page books? And the average North American only reads two good books a year. Think of the advantage that will give you over the competition in whatever the field. Caution must also be given, so as not to mistake activity with accomplishment.

This reminds me of another story I was told of an experiment done by Jean Henri Fabre (1823-1915) one of the world's greatest naturalists, who is considered by many to be the father of modern entomology. Fabre spent many years studying "Prococessionary Caterpillars". He was an observer.

Fabre observed that when caterpillars left their nest to go in search of food, they would travel in a line, head to tail, head to tail ... like a miniature train trailing the thread of silk left behind by the leading caterpillar. Now, there is nothing special about the lead caterpillar: it just happens to be the one at the front.

Fabre tested out this unique behaviour with a simple experiment in which he coaxed a chain of caterpillars around a flowerpot. Each Caterpillar in the circle simply followed the threads laid by those ahead of it. He then placed the caterpillars' favourite food in the middle of the circle.

Six days later, the caterpillars were still circling and totally ignoring the pile of food. After a week of mindless activity, the caterpillars started to die from starvation and exhaustion. With an abundance of food less than six inches away, they starved to death. They confused activity with accomplishment. Result is the name of the game, but in order to get results, we have to have clearly specified identifiable objectives.

The best way to have specific, clearly identifiable objectives is to set goals. Without goals it's easy to let life reduce to "just getting by" and we all have a choice in life: To either get by and settle to exist; or to strive for a higher, sophisticated life. You must work on your goals. Many people work hard on their jobs, but do not work hard on their future. Don't let that be you. People who fail to plan, plan to fail. The future does not get better by hope; it gets better with a plan.

Remember these ten two letter words: If it is to be, it is up to me.

CHAPTER SIX
GOALS

FIRST, WE have to define the word "goal": A goal is a desired result a person or a system is working to achieve. Unless you have clearly defined goals, you cannot realize the maximum potential that lies within you. When you have goals you begin to find talents and abilities you never knew you had.

James Cash Penny (1875-1971) the founder of JC Penny Department Store once said: "Give me a stock clerk with a goal and I'll give you a man who will make history. Give me a man with no goals and I'll give you a stock clerk."

What would you think of a captain at the helm of a ship who tells his crew to shove off and set sail without having any destination or goal in mind?

I think you will agree with me that if the ship gets out of the harbour at all, it will drift aimlessly like a rudderless ship controlled by the winds and waves and perhaps ending up on a deserted beach or caught on the rocks.

You cannot drift your way to the top of the mountain. You must set goals. Goals create activity; activity as you work towards reaching them creates the excitement you need to accomplish your objective.

The psychologist put it this way: "Logic will not change an emotion, but action will."

Goals must be detailed and written down. You must have both long-range goals for the future and short-range goals for the present. Goals are like magnets; the more clearly they are defined, the harder they pull. You must be able to see your goal. It has to be detailed. You must know how it looks and feels like in your mind.

Set goals like an adult, with intelligence, but believe like a child in faith. If it means cutting out pictures and making a scrapbook just to get you to envision exactly what you want, then do just that. Part the mechanism in which goals work is to impress your subconscious mind what it is that you want, but in order to do this effectively the details must be clear. Clarity is power. (The mind and the power of the mind and the mechanism in which they work both in the physical and in the spirit realm will have to be explained in detail in another meeting.)

Seeing as this is an introduction to personal development, I will attempt to explain the basic facts regarding the way the mind functions. The mind is one, but seems to function in two separate forms: the Conscious and the subconscious. The conscious form is the aware and the personal side; the subconscious is the unaware and the impersonal side. It is the side by which faith works. Whatever impresses the conscious and in turn impresses the subconscious, must express itself in our world and in our lives as an experience.

Each idea you conceive in the conscious mind is like a seed. If you believe it and impress it upon your subconscious, it is like planting a seed in a fertile soil. It should be noted that just like the fertile soil, the mind doesn't care what you plant in it: a concrete goal or fear. The mind doesn't care and just like the fertile soil, the mind will return what you plant. Just like the seed in the soil would need some care and action in order to yield a harvest, the subconscious mind from day to day would tell us how to care for the seed in our mind and what actions to take in order to bring about the fulfilment of our dreams. These instructions usually come in the form of urges and feelings and our part is to respond with confidence and do whatever we are led to do. All this is based on natural laws.

> *I bargained with life for a penny,*
> *And life would pay no more,*
> *However I begged at evening*
> *When I counted my scanty store.*
>
> *For life is a just employer,*
> *He gives you what you ask,*
> *But once you have set the wages,*
> *Why, you must bear the task.*
>
> *I worked for a menial's hire,*
> *Only to learn dismayed,*
> *That any wage I had asked of life,*
> *Life would have willingly paid.*
>
> *Jessie B. Rittenhouse*
> *(1869-1948)*

You are guided by your mind. Don't let procrastination steal the gifts of the world that need to be delivered through you. Procrastination is a thief of generation. Stop postponing destiny. The world needs you, what you have done in the past is nothing compared to what you can do.

The estimate from researchers and scientist in this field tell us that humans are operating on about 10 percent of their mind power. What they don't tell us is that we are also experiencing about 10 percent of the joy and 10 percent of the life we are created to live.

My mentor once taught that the major value on reaching a goal is not to have the goal, but rather the person you have become to acquire it. My mentor told me it's a worthwhile objective to become a millionaire.

Not for the money, he said. "The major reason is the person you have to become to acquire it."

After you reach the goal, you can give the money away, but you will forever retain the person you have become. Once you become the person it takes to achieve a goal, the goal is no longer the most important value. The most important value is the person you became to acquire it. This is why when you suffer a temporary loss on your journey, it shouldn't get you down, because things can be replaced at any time: who you become in the process is what's permanent. When the "things" are gone, you realize that you aren't gone. You still have the skills, the awareness, the mental value; whatever it took for you to acquire those possessions is the greater value

The world has been focused on the inequality gap between the richest one percent and the rest of the world for good reasons. Such as the "super-rich elite" influencing the government policies for selfish reasons and the effect on middle class spending that is reduced and in turn fewer taxes are paid and a downward spiral begins. I get all of that, but I also find a lot of people have now begun to use it as an excuse, they have now stopped working on themselves as a way to increase in value and blame someone else for not being where they want to be.

I believe that greed and injustice needs to be chased with everything into a small corner, but I also believe that we must teach people to go to work primarily on themselves and create value. If you know your worth, then you can go get your worth and pay the price. Go through the challenges and be victorious, do not spend all day blaming others.

In the words of Napoleon Hill (1883-1970): "Success requires no explanation- Failure permits no alibis."

Most of the so-called one percent got there by creating value and serving the multitude and anyone can do that. Service to many isn't something reserved only for the rich and famous. We have been all blessed with 24 hours; however, our compensation is largely connected to what value we create with that time. If the entire wealth of the world was distributed evenly, I believe they would still somehow end up in the same hands that have them now. This is primarily because of who they have become, the skill they have learnt the experiences they have been through.

Once you understand where the true values are, you use goals not just to reach the goals; you use goals as an enticement to become a better person. You want to reap the harvest, not just for the harvest and what you can get, but also for whom you have to become to acquire it. Do it for the skills you have to develop; for the patience it takes; for the brains; and for the discipline for the leadership it builds.

You see anyone can be part of the top one percent of the world, but the way to do it is to be an enterprising person. It isn't the harvest that has the most value; the most value is the skill, the person, the personality, and the discipline. All the things you have to become to acquire the harvest becomes the primary value.

Now it's much easier to get up in the morning because you're going to work on the person you need to become. You can't make it as a wondering generality; you must become a meaningful specific.

Frank Lloyd Wright (1867-1959) said: "No stream rises higher than its source. Whatever man might build could never express or reflect more than he was. He could record neither more nor less than he had learnt of life when the buildings were built."

Caution: Setting goals, wanting a harvest, ambition, all these are great in themselves, but in our quest to the higher life, we must be careful not to sell out.

One powerful truth about goals: Your goals should never violate the laws of God or the rights of your fellow man. Do not go for something that would cost you your virtue or your values or sell out your principals. The story of Judas Iscariot of old should serve as a warning of this. According to the New Testament, Judas was one of the twelve apostles of Jesus Christ and the son of Simon Iscariot. We remember him today not for his greatness or for achieving great goals, but infamously for his kiss and betrayal of Jesus for a bribe of "thirty pieces of silver" to arresting soldiers of the High

Priest Caiaphas, who then turned Jesus over to Pontius Pilate's soldiers. The story goes on to tell us that after he received his reward, he was unhappy with himself and went on to give the money to the chief priest and elders and then hanged himself. On your journey to the higher life, remember that you will become unhappy with the person you become if you sell out. All the gold and silver in the world would not make it worth giving up your soul.

Back to setting goals and maximizing our abilities ... I will share with you two stories to help you understand that there is no limitation that can be placed on life and our abilities when faced with challenges.

The first is a story of a man by the name Dashrath Manjhi, born in 1934 to a poor labourer family of Gahlour village near Gaya, Bihar, India. In 1967, Falguni Devi, Dashrath's wife, was injured and needed immediate medical attention. Unfortunately the nearest town with a doctor was 70 kilometres away, and to get there was an arduous trek along a mountain path. As a result, his wife died due to lack of timely medical treatment.

In memory of his wife, Dashrath wanted to create a proper path to make it easier for villagers to travel to town. He dogged through the mountains. People called him "mad" but he continued to work hard and carved out a 360 feet long, 30 feet high and 25 foot-wide passage through the Gehlour Hills. It took him 22 years from 1960 to 1982 to fulfil his self-imposed task, but it granted him immortality. He finally cut down the distance from the mountains to the hospital from 70 kilometres to 15 kilometres. Dashrath finished this epic project in 1988 and this Bihari old man, Dashrath Manjhi, is today known as the "Mountain Man".

When I read stories like this it makes me understand that there is no limitation that can be placed on life; there are people who are going to see the obstacles and mountains in front of them and let that dictate their circumstances and there are others that will break down the mountains.

The second story is funny; it's about a rich man who had only one daughter. When the daughter was of marriage age, the father sent news around town that all the eligible young men should come out on a particular day to compete in a test which would determine who was fit to marry her.

On that set day, all the able-bodied young men came out. Some came with certificates and accolades and others with long extensive portfolios.

The rich man took them to his swimming pool and addressed the men: "Any of you who can swim from one end of this swimming pool to the other will marry my daughter. In addition, I'll give him 250 million dollars, a brand new car, and a house so they can start of life well. I shall be waiting to meet my son-in-law at the other side. Good luck!"

As the young men, all very excited at the prospect of winning, started taking off their shirts, a helicopter flew over and dropped snakes and crocodiles into the pool.

All the men turned back and put on their clothes again. Disappointed, some of them said, "He can go ahead and marry his daughter!"

All of a sudden, they heard a splash in the pool. Everybody watched in amazement as one gentleman struggled his way across, avoiding the snakes and crocodiles. Finally, panting, he made it to the other side as the would-be in-law.

The rich man could not believe it. He asked the man to name anything he wanted. The man was still panting uncontrollably. Finally, he got himself together and made his request saying, "Show me the person who pushed me into the pool."

When we have a reason to achieve a goal, and we have no way of retreat, we more often than not, achieve that goal one way or another.

CHAPTER SEVEN
YOUR WHY

People are always blaming their circumstances for what they are. I don't believe in circumstances. The people who get on in this world are the people who get up and look for the circumstances they want, and if they can't find them, make them.

George Bernard Shaw
(1856-1950)

Why /(h)wí/: Noun – a reason or explanation.

FIND SOMETHING within, that will push you and self-motivate you. Your "why" has to be bigger than you. When you find your why, you find a way to make the impossible, possible

They say we all face challenges in life and sometimes we get knocked down. The question asked: "Then who gets up?" It's not the potential of the individual and it's not the genetics: it's the perseverance, the person who has a big enough why.

Self-education works best when you understand your why for living. That's what motivates you to endure any "how". Life can get challenging and it will get challenging sometimes, but it's understanding your why for living, your purpose that will keep you going.

Self-education, setting goals and self-motivation will keep your fire burning. My mentor once said to me: "Catch on fire with your passion and people will come from miles to watch you burn".

As I see it, you have to be passionate about living, you have to see pass challenges for there is a time and season for everything under the heavens. You have to be self-motivated; you have to find your purpose within because life will challenge you; not to break you, but to find out how badly you want to grow. Challenges bring about growth. Just like many things in nature, a seed has to break down for new life to grow and the human muscle has to break down during exercise for a new and stronger muscle to grow. Challenges helps us become better and stronger; remember it's all about the person you are becoming.

We all get challenged, it's not a special opportunity reserved for the weak or the poor; it is a test and just like James "Buster" Douglas (b. 1960) in 1990, you need to give life all you got and fight back.

Buster Douglas had the odds against him going into a fight with invincible "Iron Mike Tyson". Beside the fact that Iron Mike was the undefeated and undisputed heavyweight champion of the world with 37 wins up to that point, Buster separated from his wife and 23 days before the fight and he suddenly lost his mother, Lula Pearl, to a stroke. We would have excused him if he lost, but instead of sulking Buster found clarity of purpose, he found his "why". He didn't let life's challenges rub him of the potential joy of living. He converted his challenges into a source of motivation to achieve his potential. And in round 10, for the first time in his career, the invincible Iron Mike Tyson was knocked down. Buster became the undisputed heavyweight champion in one of the biggest upsets in the history of sports.

During the post-fight interview, when asked how he was able to win the fight, Douglas broke down with tears down his cheeks and said: "Because of my mother ... God bless her heart."

Friedrich Nietzsche (1844-1900) once said: "If you know the why, you can live any how."

You see what your why does for you is that it reminds you that you can't give up. It reminds you that you can't quit. You why gives you a focus.

When you hear the name Raymond Anthony Lewis Jr., (b. 1975) you think of success and fame; one of the greatest linebackers in the history of the National Football League (NFL); Super Bowl Most Valuable Player, NFL defensive player of the year, selected to 13 Pro Bowls. But for most of his life his pain served as a major influence for his passion. Ray Lewis had a tough childhood. His mother was 16 years old when he was born and his father was in jail for the first nine months after his birth: and later absent for the most part of Ray's life.

Lewis had every reason to give up and he had every reason to be excused for failure, but he took the challenge and pain as a reason to succeed. Once, in 1990 a coach looking to motivate Ray handed him a year book from 1975 that listed the school's athletic records: and in there were records set by his father. He resolved to train so hard and erase all of his father's records. In his senior year, he became his high school's first all-state wrestler.

I once heard Ray Lewis speak and he said growing up he didn't like where he was, so he promised himself, his mum, and his sister that they would move out and never return. Sports was an escape for him, it taught him discipline and how to really connect within. Then he focused on "the grind". He didn't take any days off; there was no such thing as a break.

You've got to be hungry; greatness is not for the weak and uncommitted. Sometimes it's going to hurt. The key is to resolve.

Benjamin Disraeli once said: "Nothing can resist a human will that will stake even its existence on its stated purpose. Promise yourself you will never give up until you maximize your potential."

I'm going to tell you another little story.

It's about a man who wanted to know the secret of success, and decided to find out from a known guru. The guru was a wise old man who knew every secret of life. He lived quite isolated up on a mountain and so the young man set out on his quest to meet the wise old guru. On his way he faced obstacles, but he was determined to meet the guru.

Fighting his way through the forest and scaling boulders, determinedly he went on to the top. At last he reached the peak and lay on the ground gasping for air. When he got up, the guru was there seated in deep meditation.

Silently, he waited for the old man to open his eyes. After about an hour the guru woke up and glanced at the young man with a curious look.

Enthusiastically he asked the old man: "Oh wise and all-knowing seer, I come to you in search of the secret of success."

The guru simply stood up without replying and started walking down the hill. The young man started following him, hardly keeping up with the old man. They walked for a while and came to the edge of a lake. The water was crystal clear with the sun rising over the mountains and shining across the lake like a million little diamonds as each ray of the sun hit the surface. It was calm, serene, and cool. The guru walked knee deep into the lake and with a gesture, beckoned the young man closer and asked him to kneel down: without a question the enthusiastic young man did as he was ordered.

Suddenly, he felt himself seized by a strong hand at the back of his neck. His head was forced down under the water and held there firmly.

This is some kind of test the man thought to himself.

A minute passed and he was growing breathless. The grip on his neck hadn't weakened. Another minute crawled by and now he felt anxious. His heart was pounding heavily, the water pushed down on him from all sides, nothing made any sense anymore, his throat tightened, and his lungs were desperate for air.

He struggled to arise and the old man's grip became even stronger, pressing him further down into the water. The more he struggled the more disorientated he got. He pushed with his arms and legs but he couldn't find any leverage, for all he knew he was pushing himself further down.

The man was in a panic. He tried fighting, trying with all his energy to loosen the grip around his neck. His lungs burned for air. Seconds passed, and he felt his strength slowly weakening. He felt like he had nothing left in him to fight anymore. At that moment he thought he was going to die.

Just as he was about to give into the darkness and let the water take him, this wise guru let go.

The young man instantly rushed out of the water and onto the shore; drawing in his heavy gasps. Precious oxygen flooded his lungs. His vision gradually grew clearer; the hammering in his throat slowed down; and his hands and body gradually stopped trembling.

He felt a deep anger welling up from within him. He stood up and faced the Guru: "Are you crazy, do you want to kill me? I could have easily drowned and died!"

The Guru simply stared at him for a long moment, and then he spoke for the first time. "You come to me seeking the secret of success. There it is, pointing at the lake. A few moments ago, how badly did you want to take the next breath of air? When you want to succeed as badly as you wanted to breathe, then you'll be successful."

Without saying another word the old guru turned around, leaving the young man in deep thoughts and walked back to his mountain abode.

When you have a strong enough why, a strong enough reason, then you will begin to accomplish your goals. Reasons comes first, answers come second. Remember every dream will be tested.

CHAPTER EIGHT

SHARE

"Give and it will be given to you. A good measure, pressed down, shaken together and running over."

Luke 6:38, KJV

THE THIRD part to personal development is the ability to share our knowledge, resources, and potential.

As John Maxwell (b. 1947) said " Be a river not a reservoir."

Part of our value comes from sowing seeds into the lives of others. A story I read a while ago highlights this important concept.

To pay his way through school, an under-privileged boy was selling goods from door to door. Hungry and without cash, he decided he would ask for a meal at the next house he went to; however, he lost his nerve when a lovely young woman opened the door.

Feeling ready to give up and quit, instead of a meal the young boy asked for a drink of water. The young girl thought he looked hungry so she brought him a large glass of milk. He drank it so slowly, and then asked, "How much do I owe you?"

"You don't owe me anything," she replied. "Mother has taught us never to accept pay for a kindness."

He said, "Then I thank you from my heart."

As Howard Kelly (1858-1943) left the house, he not only felt stronger physically, but he had a renewed and strengthened faith in God and man.

Many years later the same young woman became critically ill. The local doctors were baffled. They finally sent her to the big city, where they called in a specialist to study her rare disease.

Dr. Howard Kelly was called in for the consultation. When he heard the name of the town she came from, a strange light filled his eyes. Immediately he rose and went down the hall of the hospital to her room.

Dressed in his doctor's gown he went to see her. He recognized her at once. He went back to the consultation room determined to do his best to save her life. From that day he gave special attention to her case. After a long struggle, the battle was won.

Dr. Kelly requested the hospital's administration to send the final bill to him for approval. He looked at it and wrote something on the edge before the bill was sent to the lady's room. She was afraid to open it; she was sure it would take the rest of her life to pay for it all. Finally, she looked and something caught her attention on the side of the bill. She read these words ...

Paid in full with one glass of milk.
Dr. Howard Kelly

Tears of joy flooded her eyes as her happy heart prayed: "Thank You, God, that your love has spread broad through human hearts and hands."

There's a saying, which goes something like this: "Bread cast on the waters comes back to you."

The good deed you do today may benefit you or someone you love at the least expected time. If you never see the deed again at least you will have made the world a better place - and, after all, isn't that what life is all about?

That message touched my heart and it is so true. When we help others, we help ourselves. It is one of those unique life process, it is somewhat of a paradox because the more you give, the more you receive and the more you become. When you pour out from within you, it creates the capacity for more.

I suggest that you deliberately figure out ways to share. Be a "Go-Giver". Give of your-self; give of your time; give of your under-standing; and most importantly share ideas and philosophies that have made a difference in your life. Ideas and philosophy that helped to revolutionize your life are bound to do the same for others.

My mentor once said he built his life by this philosophy: "Help enough people get what they want, and you will get everything you want." You don't have to start with 100, start with one. If you want to achieve your goals, help others achieve theirs.

He who wishes to be the greatest in wealth or in personal growth must find a way to be the servant of many. The law says: "If you plant, you will reap."

In your own enlightened self-interest, develop a habitual concern about, "How can I give?" When you withhold from others that which is good and desirable, your own portion of the good and desirable diminishes.

Lao-Tzu (604BC-531BC) said: "Kindness in words creates confidence. Kindness in thinking creates profoundness. Kindness in giving creates love."

The greatest of these is love as we are reminded of in the Bible.

CONCLUSION
CHANGE YOUR WORLD

"To avoid criticism, do nothing, say nothing, and be nothing."

Louis Ellet Hubbard
(1862-1914)

PERSONAL GROWTH accompanied by understanding your purpose and making measurable progress towards it is not an easy task. Creating a life worth living is a challenge. Developing to the full extent of your potential is a challenge and you may have to deal with disappointment; however, with this price is the promise of a unique life.

And, I am warning you that some people will laugh at you when you begin this journey of personal growth. However, as my mentor once said: "No one has ever erected a stature in honour of a critic."

He reminded me when Robert Fulton (1765-1815) went steaming by in his steamboat on the Hudson River; the Wright Brothers who made that historic flight; Alexander Graham Bell who made a phone call that opened the lines of communication; and many other visionaries whose work has become so important today. People might laugh as you set out to grow; however, the real supporters will be there for you at the finish line cheering you as you cross. . Remember to stay around people that will empower you as you move into the process of transformation and personal growth.

"Without ambition one starts nothing. Without work one finishes nothing. The prize will not be sent to you. You have to win it."

Ralph Waldo Emerson (1803-1882)

If you want to the future to change, you have to change. If you will change, work on yourself and create something of value, everything will change for you. Remember, it is a person who must determine their value to themself and their world.

As Albert Einstein (1879-1955) said: "Strive not to be a success, but rather to be of value."

All the necessary ingredients to greatness are in everyone but the degree of greatness you will achieve will depend only on the extent to which you develop yourself to bring your real powers to bear.

SP Sherman (1823-1900) once said: "In the days of one's youth and ones period of apprenticeship it is of far more importance to make oneself an effective instrument than to know how or where the instrument is to be used; tamper the iron, sharpen the blade and be rest assured the world will use it."

The fact is: living the life of your dreams is possible. People prove that every day. Each and every day there are people all around the world who are living their dreams. Someone somewhere is going to improve their life; so why not let it be you?

Resolve today to make the best of your time here on Earth, to live your life to its full potential. Change and grow and your world will change for you. I wish for you all the good things that come from paying the price.

Printed in Canada